KIDS THROUGHOUT HISTORY™

Kids in Ancient Rome

Lisa A. Wroble

The Rosen Publishing Group's
PowerKids Press™
New York

Published in 1999 by The Rosen Publishing Group, Inc.
29 East 21st Street, New York, NY 10010

First Edition

Book Design: Danielle Primiceri

Photo Credits: Cover, pp. 4, 11, 19, 20 © Corbis-Bettmann; pp. 7, 8 © Scala/Art Resource; pp.12, 15 © Archive Photos; p.16 by Gustave Boulanger, provided by Corbis-Bettmann.

Wroble, Lisa A.
    Kids in Ancient Rome / by Lisa A. Wroble.
        p.   cm.—(Kids throughout history)
    Includes index.
    Summary: Discusses the food, dress, schooling, games, housing, and culture of children in Ancient Rome.
    ISBN 0-8239-5253-3
    1. Children—Rome—Juvenile literature. 2 Family—Rome—Juvenile literature. 3. Rome—Social life and customs—Juvenile literature. [1. Rome—Civilization.] I. Title. II. Series: Wroble, Lisa A.
    Kids throughout history.
    DG91.W75 1998
    305.23'0937—dc21
                                            97-32288
                                              CIP
                                              AC

Manufactured in the United States of America

Contents

The Roman Empire

Roman times were a period in history from 300 BC to 400 AD. They lasted about 700 years. The Roman **Empire** (EM-pyr) included half of Europe, most of the Middle East, and the northern coast of Africa. People across the Empire were protected by the Roman army. Laws kept large cities orderly and safe. Families, education, and healthy living were important to the people in the Empire. Modern times have a lot in common with Roman times.

◀ *The way we live now has a lot to do with how the ancient Romans lived.*

Cities

Roman cities were large and crowded. Most shops were grouped together in one area of the city. Houses were built so close together that the walls often touched. The main roads were paved. Others were made of hard-packed dirt. At the center of the city was an open area called the **forum** (FOR-um). Men gathered at the forum to hear speeches and hold meetings. Temples and city office buildings were built around the edges of the forum. A wall around the city kept everyone safe from enemies.

This model of ancient Rome shows what this important city once looked like. ▶

Good Designers

Marcus was a Roman boy. He dreamed of becoming an **engineer** (en-jin-EER). He wanted to design and build roads, buildings, and water systems. The engineers who built these things in Roman cities did a very good job. Some of the roads and water pipes were built so well that they are still used today! The Romans built **aqueducts** (AK-weh-dukts). These were human-made pipes that carried water from the rivers to tanks in the cities. Pumps and pipes carried water to all parts of the cities. This had never been done before.

◄ *There were many beautiful buildings in ancient Rome.*

Houses

Marcus's house was made of brick. The outside of the house was covered with plaster. Clay tiles covered the roof. Like most of the houses on his street, only the second floor of his house had windows. A **skylight** (SKY-lyt), or opening in the roof, allowed even more light into his home. One was often built over an **atrium** (AY-tree-um). An atrium usually had a pool that collected rain water. Trees and plants grown near the pool created an indoor garden. The family's bedrooms and the living room were located around the atrium.

The atrium was often a central place in the home where families gathered. ▶

Clothing

Roman people wore large, loose shirts called **tunics** (TOO-niks) that were belted around the waist. Tunics often hung to the knees. Marcus and his father wore **togas** (TOH-guhz) over their tunics. A toga was a long cloth that draped over one shoulder and wrapped around the body. Women and girls wore **stolas** (STOH-luhz). A stola was an ankle-length tunic with a belt at the waist and another one around the chest. Most people wore leather sandals.

◀ *Most of the clothes that Romans wore were made out of wool or linen.*

Food

Marcus and his family ate together in the main living room. This room was called the **tablinum** (TAB-len-um). They would often lie back on long, wide couches to eat. They propped themselves up on their elbows. Two or three people shared a couch. Foods, such as grapes, olives, figs, eggs, fish, and bread, were placed on a low table. Marcus and his family took food from the serving bowls and, like other Romans, ate it with their fingers.

Wine mixed with water and a little bit of honey was also served at meals.

The plates and bowls used in ancient Rome are similar to those we use today. ▶

Families

Families were important in Roman times and family members spent a lot of time with each other. They ate, played games with dice, and told stories together. Boys often wrestled and played with marbles. Girls played with dolls. Both boys and girls liked to play a game of rolling large hoops with a stick. Families went together to horse races and watched plays at the theater. Marcus especially liked to hear music at the theater.

◀ *A house's atrium was a popular place for Roman children to play.*

Education

Like many children, Marcus started school when he was seven years old. He learned to speak, read, and write Latin. Latin was the language of the ancient Romans. He practiced writing on a wax tablet, which could be scraped smooth and used again. At the age of twelve, Marcus would begin to learn Roman history, math, and **astronomy** (uh-STRON-uh-mee). Girls went to school until they were twelve. Then they stayed home and learned how to weave and sew.

Teachers in ancient Rome taught their students many of the same subjects that kids study today. ▶

Religion

Ancient Romans believed that beings greater than humans called gods and goddesses controlled everything in the world. Each god or goddess governed a different thing, such as the ocean or crops. When Marcus asked a favor of a goddess, he left an offering, such as a coin or food. He also left offerings to thank the gods when a favor was granted. Each city and family had its own god or goddess for protection. He or she was chosen by the head of the city or the family. **Festivals** (FES-tih-vulz) were held each year in honor of the god of the city.

Each day, prayers and offerings were made to the household gods and goddesses.

Social Life

Many things we do today were actually started during the Roman Empire. Families and education are very important now, as they were then. We still have discussions in public places, much the same as in the Roman forums. We have water pumped into our homes through pipes. We also use **sewer systems** (SOO-er SIS-temz), just like those in ancient Rome. And children study some of the same subjects and play many of the same games that Marcus and his friends did. We have learned a lot from the ancient Romans.

Glossary

aqueduct (AK-weh-dukt) A channel or pipe used to carry water long distances.

astronomy (uh-STRON-uh-mee) The study of the planets and stars.

atrium (AY-tree-um) An indoor garden.

empire (EM-pyr) A group of nations under one ruler.

engineer (en-jin-EER) A person who designs things that we use.

festival (FES-tih-vul) A day or special time of recognizing someone or something important.

forum (FOR-um) An open area where speeches are given and meetings are held.

sewer system (SOO-er SIS-tem) An underground system of pipes that carries away waste.

skylight (SKY-lyt) An opening or window in the roof.

stola (STOH-luh) A long tunic worn by women and girls.

tablinum (TAB-len-um) The main living and dining room in a Roman home.

toga (TOH-guh) A long piece of cloth wrapped around the body that was worn by men and boys.

tunic (TOO-nik) A large, loose shirt.

Index